COVID Dissonance

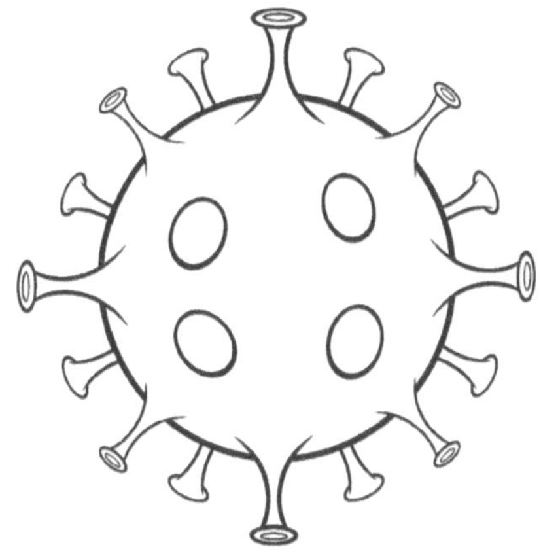

Jennifer Lagier

Cyberwit.net
HIG 45 Kaushambi Kunj, Kalindipuram
Allahabad - 211011 (U.P.) India
http://www.cyberwit.net
Tel: +(91) 9415091004
E-mail: info@cyberwit.net

Printed at Thomson Press India Limited.

"This reckless indifference is costing people their lives. And it is past time that we start protecting each other and taking this seriously because thanks to these guys, the Knucklehead Hall of Fame is getting pretty fucking crowded."

- John Oliver

Contents

Masked 7

Faux News 8

Thinning the Herd 9

Ignition 11

Illumination 12

Entry 13

Pandemic 14

Strategies for Surviving tRump Virus 15

Hidden Blessings 16

Flow 17

Mass Delusion 18

Sheltering 19

Stick Houses 20

Pandemic Needs 21

Appreciation of the Minuscule 22

Boundaries 23

Quarantine Prayer 24

COVID Coiffure 25

Pandemic Pastimes 26

Smudge 27

Pandemic Thanksgiving 28

COVID Dissonance 29

Chained Maiden 30

Cloud Angel 31

Morning Walker 32

About the Author 33

Acknowledgments 34

Books by Jennifer Lagier 35

Masked

Swathed in cotton scarf, latex gloves,
only inches of skin remain uncovered.
I prepare for walks like an astronaut
about to exit protective capsule,
fragile body ejected into perilous space.

Grocery shopping was once an exercise
in selecting unblemished fruit. organic vegetables,
visiting with cashiers and neighbors.
Now it is the equivalent of the hunger games,
all of us unwilling tributes, trying to survive
newly lethal environment.

I am the invisible woman,
possibly a bank robber, cattle rustler,
or tempting seductress,
my expression inscrutable as I venture forth
beneath cloaking mask.

Faux News

Propaganda bots gaslight,
spew disinformation that jeopardizes
health, sanity, nation.
David Plouffe accuses talking heads
of providing Cretin-in-Chief
his own media Westworld.

During a TV interview,
IMPOTUS III urges sick Americans
to report to work as he
considers coronavirus mild,
not pandemic, just a public relations threat
dreamed up by disgruntled Democrats.

The butcher's bill rises,
stock market crashes.
Retailers sell out of masks and Purell.
New infections multiply, fatalities burgeon.
Test kits are flawed and in short supply,
WHO doctors contradicted, CDC muzzled.

Thinning the Herd

*"A community achieves herd immunity against a certain dis-
ease when a high enough proportion of people are immune to
the pathogen that causes it, either because they have been vac-
cinated or because they have previously been exposed."*
– Newsweek

Three days into self-quarantine, a meme
showing one of the four horsemen of the apocalypse
hoarding toilet paper no longer brings laughs.

Grocery stores ration hand sanitizers, water
as panic buying runs off the rails.
Public schools and offices close.
Community events are cancelled/rescheduled.
Social distancing is the new reality
in entertainment venues and gyms.

IMPOTUS III flaunts his exposure
to coronavirus-19, refuses to lay low
or be tested, holds a series
of increasingly deranged press conferences
where journalists have their temperatures checked
prior to admittance, mics cut if they ask questions
that highlight incompetence.

Trumpanzis claim it's all a hoax,
defy CDC warnings, ridicule prudent instructions
on wearing masks to stay safe.
The rest of us remain home, welcome free time

as we observe pandemic spread of lethal contagion
which validates Darwin's theories,
thins the ignorant herd.

Ignition

"Stars collided and collapsed.
Fire was the uninvited guest."
~ Barbara Quick

Like cave-dwelling ancestors,
we huddle for warmth
by a crackling fire,
hide from pandemic virus,
trust isolation will save us.

Outside, panic erupts
as terrified herds
clean off grocery store shelves,
hoard water, toilet paper, sanitizer,
more than they could use in a lifetime.

The economy crashes, infection rates burgeon,
death counts trend upward.
Rumors ignite zombie apocalypse.
Civilization burns to the ground.
Social norms fracture.

Illumination

"Walking, I vanish into light."
~ Jack Foley, "Kore"

Skies split and spatter.
Housebound captives fret until
storm clouds disperse, reveal radiance.

I emerge, hike among bruised eucalyptus,
shoes powdered with yellow pollen
from battered acacia.

Later, I tug dandelions from sodden mulch,
tidy overgrown flower beds,
dead-head daffodils, pluck calla lilies.

Sunbeams illuminate poppies,
blue and white lupine spires,
chiaroscuro stripes of covenant rainbow.

Entry

"Sometimes we stare so long at a door that is closing that we see too late the one that is open." — *Alexander Graham Bell*

The original front entry was yellow, bore scratches,
signs of abuse by the former inhabitants,
solid wood, a struggle to open or close.

I tried scrubbing scuff marks, painting over gouges,
finally gave up, consulted with a handyman
and Home Depot salesmen for its replacement.

The first four-paneled fiberglass version
arrived with hinges and knob holes
cut into the wrong side and was returned.

The second was less expensive,
but came with correct configuration,
was installed with minimum fuss.

Now, fearing contagion, we shelter in place
behind secure portal where I give thanks
this new door contains glass, admits welcome light.

Pandemic

*"It's not death we fear but that things won't be the same." —
Joan Colby*

While sheltering in place, we tell ourselves
this is Mother Nature's time out,
house arrest for a population
oblivious to what plastic,
chemicals, overconsumption
do to our bodies and planet earth.

Contagion and death counts escalate.
Self-serving politicians on both sides of the aisle
manipulate the stock market,
crash the economy to make a killing,
deny medical supplies, earmark billions
for a corporate slush fund.

Abandoned on the battlefield,
we've been told to trust optimistic misinformation,
Lord of the Flies guidelines to saving ourselves.
Dark memes provide gallows humor.
A skeletal horseman gallops toward apocalypse,
unopened packs of toilet paper under both bony arms.

Strategies for Surviving tRump Virus

Shelter in place.
When venturing forth to buy groceries,
wear gloves and a mask.
Stay six to ten feet away from others.
Wash every stitch of clothing
as soon as you're home.
Clean every surface with disinfectant.
Carry Chlorox wipes in the car.
Wash hands constantly.
Do not touch your face.
Shun crowds like the plague.
Be grateful you can afford delivery services.
Order take out/curbside pickup at least once a week.
Confer with your doctor via web-based video.
Try not to binge overeat.
Keep busy to avoid going insane.
Give your cranky husband plenty of space.
Exercise, work in the garden.
Read all those books on your shelves.
Attend Zoom support group meetings.
Ration exposure to Internet news.
Eschew clueless television talking heads.
Avoid obsessing over rising infection and death rates.
Subject yourself to antibody testing.
Tell yourself things will someday improve.
Persuade friends to call out conspiracy theories, lies.
In November, demand change and vote.

Hidden Blessings

As we shelter in place,
nature regenerates eroded ozone.
Deer and mountain lions reclaim community parks.
Highways are empty,
Sushi Heaven shuttered.

Quarantine gives us space
for meditation, reconnecting with earth.
The Pacific soothes, sluices ashore,
sprinkles the beach with broken sand dollars,
feathers, frayed sections of rope.
Ocean waves reshape granite headlands,
smooth jagged rock into polished moonstones.

In the bay, whales spout and breach,
shelter their calves before heading south.
Over Fisherman's Wharf,
blackbirds wrangle with seagulls.
Tides rise and fall.
Daylight cycles into darkness.
Sunrise returns.

Flow

Dew sprinkles droplets from receding fog,
bejewels bronze chrysanthemums.
Coffee wafts an inviting aroma
as scalding water saturates grounds,
fills waiting carafe.
Dogs grumble, paw the front door,
eager to be taken outside.

Invisible contagion surges.
Months of sheltering in place leave my hair
shaggy and silver, fingernails unpainted, soul restive.
Busy work offers the illusion of control,
pretense of normal routines during spreading pandemic.
I dead-head Peruvian lilies, strip yellowed foliage
from past-their-prime foxgloves, blotchy geraniums.

Surrounded by hummingbirds and salvia,
I breathe in pungent scent of herbal chaparral,
perform familiar garden tasks.
Industry soothes.
Hands pull weeds, pick purple and orange gladiolus.
I cultivate serenity, savor this safe realm.
Gratitude flows.

Mass Delusion

Instead of wearing a mask
practicing social distancing,
Mango Mussolini insists
on conducting Nuremberg Rallies.

Red-hatted acolytes crowd together,
scoff at science, statistical evidence,
spread viral infection,
fuel ongoing pandemic.

Sceptics quote discredited physicians,
frame caution as cowardice,
refer to those who follow CDC guidelines
as simpleton sheeple.

They pack the beaches,
converge on tourist towns,
return to bars, tattoo parlors,
gather in churches.

Infection rates skyrocket.
Body counts burgeon.
If this is a cosmic IQ test,
our country is failing.

Sheltering

"Protect or shield from something harmful."

Two years ago, we inhabited
a cramped two-story Marina townhouse
surrounded by demoralizing fog,
frail, tottering cypress.

Today I am grateful
for the sunny Monterey home
where we live now,
plenty of high-ceilinged rooms
within which to isolate,
protect ourselves from pandemic virus.

My corner lot features drought tolerant garden,
planter beds burgeoning with white lilies,
yellow jonquils, golden nasturtium.
Backyard barrel halves spill orange hibiscus,
purple bougainvillea, fragrant pink roses.
Lavender wisteria pulls itself up pergola beams,
clings to wooden slat awning.

In cozy office, I scribble
serenaded by streaming zen music,
realize sheltering in place is the gift
of being an artist in residence,
not incarceration.

Stick Houses

"Little pig, little pig, let me come in."
"No, not, by the hair on my chinny chin chin."
"Then I'll huff, and I'll puff, and I'll blow your house in."

Sheltering in place,
we starve for companionship,
crave freedom, calm ourselves with walks
six feet apart along cleansing surf.

During morning meanders,
I give thanks for wild iris, gold poppies,
appreciate lace-edged turquoise waves
as they wash granite shoreline.

Despite pandemic, some still gather,
scorn social distancing, hug in greeting,
wander four abreast
along skinny trail.

At Carmel River Lagoon,
an anonymous architect constructs
rustic sticks-and-stone cottage,
evokes little pigs who made fatal choices.

Pandemic Needs

Health care workers, first responders
require protective masks, HazMat clothing,
respirators for the critically ill.

Weekly, I suit and glove up, cover nose and mouth,
take advantage of senior hour at the grocery,
purchase needed bread, meat, produce.

I crave morning walks along sand dunes,
meditations among cypress,
wildflower vistas, fresh ocean air.

A goddess support network
sustains this poet's soul.
Wry online cartoons make me laugh.

Daily, I practice patience,
acceptance of circumstances
over which I have no power.

Appreciation of the Minuscule

Red-headed hummingbirds
materialize during twilight,
whirr among scarlet salvia,
defend fragrant territory,
buzz like disturbed bees.

Within shadows, purple wisteria bud,
dangle immature blossoms,
collapsed Chinese lanterns.
Tiny bats pass before full moon,
disappear into darkness.

Skunks and raccoons emerge,
patrol nocturnal sanctuary,
slink beneath windowsills,
nest within hydrangeas,
hardy pink vinca.

Baby possums cautiously teeter
across ragged fence line
as night draws its ebony curtain.
We shelter to evade unseen perils.
Minuscule tree frogs soothingly croon.

Boundaries

As we shelter in place,
spring accessorizes sand dunes
with lavender lupine,
spatters of golden poppies,
scarlet Indian paintbrush.

Social distancing is state ordered,
subject to citation, fines,
a matter of life and death.
Masked and gloved, thirteen feet apart,
we pass on sidewalks and trails.

Nursing home visits are conducted
through heavily screened windows
or on computers equipped with
microphones, cameras and Zoom.
Loved ones can't understand, languish alone.

During mandatory time out,
we accept confined life's slower pace.
I scribble poetry, clean closets, bake bread,
appreciate garden and books
while we isolate, flatten contagion's curve.

Quarantine Prayer

Deer and raccoons reclaim sidewalks and streets
while quarantined humans shelter in place.

Given an existential time out,
I meditate on acts of community kindness:
neighbors who deliver groceries and prescriptions
to vulnerable housebound.

Each day offers more blessings:
health, cherished garden, hummingbird angels.
I deadhead lilies, plant cosmos seedlings,
strip away stinging nettles.

Grateful for husband and hounds,
well-stocked pantry and freezer,
I bake fragrant artisan bread,
simmer bolognese sauce, pour over pasta.

Sustaining goddess of hearth and home,
may your protective powers surround us.

COVID Coiffure

After months of sheltering in place,
hair salons shuttered,
my manicured coif loses shape,
reverts to lengthening plaits
of white, silver, gold.

My husband's bald spot enlarges.
To distract the eye
from thinning scalp fringe,
straggling gray wisps
approaching his shoulders,
he cultivates a snowy goatee.

As shut down persists,
civil unrest escalates,
democracy falters.
During viral déjà vu,
we relive the turbulent sixties,
morph into straggly-haired hippies.

Pandemic Pastimes

My sister channels our dead mom
who alternated between feeding birds
and screaming at Jamaican telephone scammers
masquerading as social security employees
or bankers, demanding credit card numbers.

I hibernate, read poetry,
pull weeds, organize cupboards,
sweat to YouTube videos,
work out with weights in the gym
I've set up in our office.

The dogs are thrilled with constant attention,
walks around the block,
visits to the neighborhood park,
afternoon naps curled beside me
on a California King bed.

Around us, invisible virus burgeons.
Cautious, we shelter in place,
become addicted to take out, Netflix and Zoom,
still trying to guess when COVID
will be conquered and isolation ends.

Smudge

As California's central coast burns,
orange and scarlet flames outline hilltops.
Sepia skies fill with acrid reek,
rain down silver cinders.

Smoky air corrodes throat and lungs.
Outdoor diners and tables
are freckled with ashes.
Lethal pandemic keeps us inside.

Deer and mountain lions flee,
invade nearby neighborhoods,
take over parks and yards,
prey on rabbits, squirrels, trusting pets.

I shelter in an oceanside cottage
south of Hearst Castle,
watch gray flakes drift,
stick to windows and sidewalks.

Wilderness ignites, is consumed.
There is no escape from coronavirus,
rapid climate change,
toxic effects of advancing inferno.

Pandemic Thanksgiving

We've spent eight months
in self-quarantine, seniors
isolated for our protection.
Travel, live music continue without us.

In solitude, I give thanks,
compose a daily gratitude list
for continued health, loving family,
supportive friends, flourishing garden.
Sheltering in place brings free time,
domestic and spiritual renewal.

It's the opposite of incarceration:
breathing space for reflection, creation.

COVID Dissonance

"Six-foot distance and wearing masks are pagan rituals of satanic worshippers," said parent Heidi Anderson. "My kids are Christian they are not subject to wearing masks."

As schools debate in-person classes,
the cognitively challenged rise up,
wave signs, guns and bibles
to protest protection.

Eager to sacrifice children and teachers,
they embrace crackpot conspiracy theories,
swarm into public meetings, rave at the podium,
spew hatred and misinformation.

Whipped to a frenzy
by Fox News and the White House,
non-critical thinkers claim first amendment rights,
spread violence and viral infections.

Chained Maiden

"I am a cluster of bright beads
I am the farthest star"
~ N. Scott Momaday, from "The Delight Song of Tsoai-talee"

Autumn extinguishes Indian Summer.
The Andromeda Constellation freckles night sky,
recalls a king's daughter, sacrificed to sate a monster,
chained to a rock as raging Cetus ravages coastline.

We remain in semi-quarantine,
venture forth masked, gloved and cautious,
unwilling to surrender life for political statements,
forfeit our health at the altar of COVID.

Science serves as a Perseus shield,
offers protective protocols to ward off contagion.
We rely on each other for groceries, errands, comfort,
share coffee outdoors, survive the pandemic.

Cloud Angel

"I am a feather on the bright sky"
~ N. Scott Momaday, from "The Delight Song of Tsoai-talee"

Shore fog molds itself into a winged seraph
sailing across sapphire sky
above shaggy pines.

Gray pelicans soar, skim autumn ocean,
survey pleated waves,
bellyflop into anchovy shoals.

A sea gull, masquerading as spirit guide,
spirals over damp beach, drops a feather token,
leaves an angelic fragment behind.

Morning Walker

*"Of all the paths you take in life, make sure a few of them are
dirt."*   *~ John Muir*

What mystery lurks beyond tame sidewalk,
seduces the curious out of suburbia into forest,
leads the long-sheltered explorer up steep Jack's Peak path,
offers 180-degree ocean vistas?

Overhead, red-headed woodpecker percussion.
Yellow ice pick beak excavates wood beetles,
bores tiny craters into sycamores, drought-stricken pines.
Spooked deer explode from coastal oak chaparral.

This feral retreat offers off-road, elevated perspective,
backcountry meditations among soaring redwoods,
thorny blackberry tangles, puddles of sorrel.
Take the mountain lion trail. Remember freedom.
Revert to the wild.

About the Author

Dr. Jennifer Lagier has published nineteen books. Her work appears in a variety of journals, ezines and anthologies including *Fog and Light* (Blue Light Press), *Second Wind: Words & Art of Hope & Resilience, Fire and Rain: Ecopoetry of California, Missing Persons: Reflections on Dementia, Silent Screams: Poetic Journeys Through Addiction & Recovery.* She taught with California Poets in the Schools and at Hartnell College, Monterey Peninsula College, California State University, Monterey Bay, and Modesto Junior College. Currently, she edits *The Monterey Poetry Review* and helps coordinate the Monterey Bay Poetry Consortium's Second Sunday Reading Series. Visit her website, jlagier.net, and Like her Facebook page, www.facebook.com/JenniferLagier

Acknowledgments

Cover Art by Gene McCormick.

Thank you to the editors within whose publications these poems originally appeared:

"Masked," *Silver Birch Press "Wearing a Mask" Series*
"Illumination," *Lone Stars Light of the Stars Contest*
"Entry," *Silver Birch Press "My Front Door" Series*
"Pandemic," *Winedrunk Sidewalk*
"Strategies for Surviving tRump Virus," *Winedrunk Sidewalk*
"Mass Delusion," *Winedrunk Sidewalk*
"Stick Houses," *Pangolin Review*
"Boundaries," *Winedrunk Sidewalk, Rockford Review*
"Cloud Angel," *Humana Obscura*

Books by Jennifer Lagier

Meditations on Seascapes and Cypress, Blue Light Press, 2021.

Camille Comes Unglued, Cyberwit, 2020.

Dystopia Playlist, Cyberwit, 2020.

Trumped Up Election, Xi Draconis Books, 2019.

Camille Mobilizes, FutureCycle Press, 2018.

Like a B Movie, FutureCycle Press, 2018.

Harbingers, Blue Light Press, 2016.

Scene of the Crime, Evening Street Press, 2016.

Camille Abroad, FutureCycle Press, 2016.

Where We Grew Up, FutureCycle Press, 2015.

Camille Vérité, FutureCycle Press, 2014.

Penetrating the Mist, Green Fuse Poetic Arts, 2013.

Hookup with Chinaski, Paisano Press, 2013.

Agent Provacateur, Paisano Press, 2012.

Fishing for Portents, Pudding House Publications, 2008.

Mangia Syndrome, Pudding House Publications, 2004.

Second-Class Citizen, Bordigheria, Inc., 2000.

Where We Grew Up, Paisano Press, 1999.

Coyote Dream Cantos, Iota Press, 1992.